BREAKFAST FOR CHAMPIONS:

BUILDING POSITIVE SELF-CONCEPT IN KIDS

A Positive Approach to Behavior Management
For Parents and Teachers

By

J. Zink, Ph.D.

GO GET 'EM

J. Zink

Grateful Acknowledgement to

T. BRADFORD SALES

without whose editorial assistance this book
would not have been possible.

This book is for

JOE ZINK

And his children

And theirs

PROLOGUE

My father has done an outstanding job in writing a book in a field where no one has taken charge. He writes about raising children better than anyone I know. This book entitled Breakfast For Champions is so easy to read I believe a seven-year old child could read it. In fact, if the teachers or parents reading this book have trouble they should give it to their children and have the children teach them. Breakfast For Champions is witty and certainly not boring to read. My father included a number of valuable activities to help you better relate to your children.

I can honestly say after thirteen years under my father's plan, I cannot find one fault in it. I can't think of saying thank-you any other way than, "I love you, J."

Please remember to order my father's next book What To Do When Your Champion Is Out To Lunch.

Joe Zink
(Grade Seven
Center School
Manhattan Beach
California)

TABLE OF CONTENTS

Page

PROLOGUE

PART I: THE IDEA

Chapter One: The Formula for
                  Positive Self-Concept   1

Chapter Two: The Need for Positive
                  Information   11

Chapter Three: Developing a Positive
                  Message System: An
                  Ecological Approach   17

PART II: THE SKILLS

Chapter Four: Positive Listening   27

Chapter Five: Positive Talking   41

PART III: PRACTICE

Chapter Six: Tips for Parents in
                  Trouble   55

Chapter Seven: Tips for Teachers
                  in Trouble   81

Chapter Eight: Tips for Building
                  Positive Peer Messages
                  for Appropriate
                  Behavior in Kids   105

EPILOGUE: Never Too Late to Begin   121

PART I: THE IDEA

*"There is one who gives liberally,
yet he grows richer, and one
who withholds what he should give
and suffers want."*

Proverbs 11-24

*"If you are not prepared to use
positive reinforcement, you will
not get kids to behave."*

Lee Canter
Assertive Discipline

Chapter One

THE FORMULA FOR POSITIVE SELF-CONCEPT

This book pretends to be nothing more than a "how-to" manual for building a positive self-concept in children and young adults. The language I have chosen to use here is as simple and jargon free as possible. Also, by using the word "formula" in the title of this first chapter, I do not wish to imply that I have a startling new discovery to offer parents and teachers about their kids; however, there is, upon strong examination, an obvious formula for building in kids a positive way of thinking about themselves. Such positive thinking leads to self-confidence, high self-esteem, cheerful "can-do" attitudes and general success and happiness in life.

I am not a theoretician. I am a successful teacher and parent. If you are looking for some special new theory or revelation about human behavior, look elsewhere. Libraries are filled with treatises on child development. Some are extremely engaging; others are so poorly conceived that they cannot provide answers to simple questions like "why is he so moody?" or "why does she pout when I tell her to do something?" or "why does he insist on teasing his sister?"

Every child comes to know the world through a series of continuous experiences with the people in it. As a child grows, s/he experiences more people. Even minor experiences like buying ice cream from the lady behind the counter or saying hello to a friend, provide the child with important information about him/herself. If we think of this information as a continuous and never ending, we begin to understand that this constant diet of messages provides the basic nutrition which feeds a child's self-concept. (Admittedly, by using words like "diet, nutrition, and feeds" I am creating a metaphor. I do so because it is the best way I know to describe the process of self-concept growth.) To continue the metaphor – a child who is given food of little nutritional value will suffer physical (and mental) deterioration; a child who is given nutritious food will grow and develop to his/her potential. (Some say we are what we eat; I say we are, in part, what we are fed.)

For instance, children who are continually praised for their ability to read will soon form a self-concept which clearly includes the skill of reading. This happens because a series of messages given by parents and teachers help these children to regard the act of reading as pleasurable, exciting, delightful, and a good thing to do, and through this act they experience success. Thus, the skill of reading becomes part of a child's internal picture. When this happens, we can say that the child's own message system has grown to the degree that s/he can deliver his/her own positive messages for engaging in a specific behavior. Most teachers and parents, who have serious trouble with children, forget that with children the messages about the pleasure, joy, achievement, excitement, etc., of reading (or any other behavior) must come from us first. The formula, then, is simple.

POSITIVE IN/POSITIVE OUT

As a practical example of the formula (Positive In/Positive Out) let us look at a ten year old boy whose room is constantly a mess. Let us further assume he has the basic abilities to hang clothes in the closet; neatly arrange toys and games; return books to shelves; order rock, bottle cap, baseball card, and stamp collections, make his bed, and, in general, attend to all those specific behaviors necessary to maintain a neat room*. The problem is, as most parents of 10 year olds will tell you, he doesn't do any of the above.

What often ensues is a series of messages between parents and son about the room. When analyzed most of these messages contain other messages about the person for whom they are intended.

Father: "You call this a room, this is a direct hit!" Message: you are a holocaust.

Mother: "Aren't you embarrassed to live like this?" Message: you should feel guilt.

Father: "This is a sty! Do you see the rest of us living like this? When I was your age I lived in the same room with two other brothers! You live in your own private palace and you treat it like a garbage dump!" Message: you are garbage.

---

*Of course, some basic inclinations and abilities in a given child must be present for the formula to work. It is highly unlikely that a child who suffers serious and permanent neurological impairment will ever form a self-concept which includes strong reading skills. The real danger, however, lies with the parent or teacher who makes a pre-judgment about a child's inclination and abilities before sending positive messages regarding certain skills. When we say, "Well, he will never be able to . . .," we err seriously.

Mother: I refuse to go in that closet without a tetanus shot. Actually, I am afraid of what I might catch. Message: You scare me.

This kind of reaction from parents, when it produces no permanent results, frequently degenerates into shouts, threats, angry statements, further strong messages implying that something is wrong with the kid because he chooses to live according to his own needs and not according to his parents'.

This boy might become, in order to turn off the heat, a "stuffer." All items, including matchbox cars, rubberbands for his braces, geode, one sock, gum eraser, Steve Garvey "doubles," and other treasures get shoved behind drawers, in back of the bed, behind the stereo, and the closet becomes his last place of refuge – where he will make his last stand.

The total breakdown of communication and major dramatic scene comes the day his father is searching for tennis balls and ventures into "the closet" to discover the odor seeping from the piles. Then anger, threats, lecture, tears, emotional statements – the whole closet climax.

Well it doesn't have to be that way. Again, the formula: Positive In/Positive Out. If the goal is for the ten year old to internalize neatness – that is, to be uncomfortable himself when he walks into a messy room – the place for the parents to begin is with a direct communication. They could try: "We want you, Brian, to hang all clothes in the closet, put all books on the shelves, place all underwear in the drawers, or, if dirty, in the dirty clothes hamper. We want no fuzz or bits of paper on the floor."

Now comes the critical step. Remember the formula says "Positive In" first. So keep an "eagle eye" for Brian's first response to your specific message. As soon as he puts books on their shelves say: "Brian, thank you for putting your books on the shelf." Now, look him in the eye and mean it. Don't say: "Yeah, you got the books but you forgot your underwear on the floor." (This is very typical of most parents.) Instead say: "Brian, I am delighted that you thought enough of my wishes that you responded so quickly." Don't say: "Nice going, champ, but your closet still smells." Say: "Brian, I realize that it takes extra effort to put things away and that you put in the effort for me. Thank you, son. I love it." And put some passion into it. If you are not authentic in your praise of kids, they will know it immediately and they will never respect you.

When I say "Positive In," I mean positive in every sense of the word. If what you say is positive in your mind, but is interpreted by the child to be other than positive, then trouble may be the result. One nice thing about "Positive In" is that it is so pleasant to be with people who are positive. And, if you are with a positive person, your comfort is assured. Positive people do not threaten nor do they intimidate for the sake of winning at the expense of someone else. Truly positive people do not find joy in winning at someone else's expense. Remember, if you win at the expense of your child's self-concept, you have lost. Period!

We cannot discount the powerful impact of emotions in the first part of the formula "Positive In." The more positive messages that children receive the more they will begin to regard themselves in terms of those positive messages. For instance, let us return to Brian. After his parents have taken the time to convey their specific needs to Brian and they have taken the pains to carefully send him messages of goodwill and joy regarding his respect of those needs, Brian begins to understand them as people. Brian begins to realize he can make them happy by simply putting his books away and storing his underwear or toys in their proper places. After a while, (with kids whose self-concept has not been deeply negatively embedded – this time is very short, perhaps three or four days, a week, maybe two) Brian begins to think of himself as a neat person.

A word about non-verbal language is also in order (a subject discussed in-depth in later chapters). Parents and teachers often forget that up to 80% of the messages we send children are non-verbal. The point is children learn from infancy to communicate non-verbally: it takes them several years to learn what the sounds we make with our mouths mean and several more to understand what these black marks on a white page mean. But, from birth, and some argue reasonably that before birth, children are learning non-verbally.

So remember the formula – Positive In/ Positive Out. If your children at home or in your classroom are scowling at you, it may be that you are scowling at them. If, when you draw near them, their eyes narrow, or more significantly, their pupils contract, they have

learned these behaviors from you and your
body language. Change your non-verbal messages from negative to positive and use these to
reinforce your positive verbal messages to kids.
Smiles in particular are powerful non-verbal
positives. And I mean sincere smiles, not
"ah-ha, I got you now!" smiles. Try warm and
sincere messages which say, "I care about
you." Winks, laughter, a loving pat; hand-
shake between father and teenage son; baseball handslapping of victory; all expressions of
affection and caring are the kind of positive
messages that will return. When they do –
"Positive Out" – it is a sign that the child has
not only observed and received your positive
messages but that s/he feels sufficiently con-
fident to send them back.

Now, as with all new skills, sending positive messages to kids takes practice. And,
when attempting to communicate positively with
a child who has a very negative self-concept,
you cannot charge in glad-handing and back-
slapping, winking and smiling all the while. It
will not work. Worse, it will backfire and
serve to further alienate the young person.
With some it will serve to reinforce the persis-
tent notion among the young that older people
are weird, parents are square, principals are
wacko and teachers are manipulators not to be
trusted. Go gently at first. Send sincere messages and if you don't mean them, don't send
them. Kids read us the way we read books. If
your "Positive-In" is not sincere or is over-
done, you can forget about "Positive-Out."

Now a final word about the formula. The
jaundiced eye might look at this formula and
say: "Fine. All you will do is teach kids how

to please you and ultimately manipulate you for their own ends."

My response to this worthwhile objection to the formula has two parts. In the first place, positive messages coming back to us from kids is the ultimate test that the formula is working. If those messages are not authentic, then we can observe a gross discrepancy between what the kids say and what they do. Second, if the kids are so accomplished that they can match their positive words and body messages to us with positive action, then we are seeing either positive self-concept ("I told you I would get an 'A' on my next math test and here it is!") or we are witnessing a young person exercising his/her new skills at interacting and communicating. Both of these latter alternatives are exciting for parents and teachers to see.

10

Chapter Two
THE NEED FOR POSITIVE INFORMATION

Children are born with a non-existent or
very, very fragile sense of who or what they
are. Infants who are ignored but fed
regularly – who are deprived of either hardship
or loving caresses – often die. Older children
who suffer repeated rejection may build very
strong defenses around themselves for protec-
tion against rejection. Some of them commit
suicide when their defenses cave in. These, of
course, are extreme cases, but they are not
rare.

Fortunately, most children receive sufficient attention to keep them alive. If the attention is essentially positive, then they will for-
mulate a generally positive image of themselves
and they will begin to feel good about themselves. If the attention is too little and infre-
quent, then they will experiment to determine
what they must do to get attention. Stimulation
of any kind is better than none at all and some
children learn that disruption and socially mal-
adaptive behavior is extremely adaptive for
their main need – attention. These children
will not hesitate to cry in church, scream in
the airplane, throw mashed potatoes in the
restaurant or stick their finger in their little
brother's eye. All these behaviors very
quickly achieve their purpose – attention. In
the latter case, the eye poking behavior
achieves a double purpose because little brother
deserves a good poke since he's been the target
for all the available attention anyway.

Mother frequently scolds with words like,
"You have been nothing but trouble all day!"
Unfortunately self-concepts are built on such
observations. A child whose need for attention
is gratified first by the attention and then by

an observation confirming a suspicion that the only way to get anyone to notice is to raise a little hell soon thinks of him/her as an effective hell-raiser. In later years, he/she may proudly sport a tatoo that proclaims "born to raise hell."

In very simple terms, self-concept is the mental picture we have of ourselves. It includes things like our names, our backgrounds, our experiences, our sense of right and wrong, our sense of our relationship to others, our sense of God – (or the ultimate power), our understanding of love and rejection and other powerful emotions, such as what we consider "right" for us in terms of friends, ideas, cars, clothes, music, education and many, many other aspects of our lives that help us to make decisions.

The process of self-concept development and the process of how we make decisions about our behavior are very difficult to separate. Although philosophers may well argue distinctions, let us, as parents and teachers, for the sake of understanding our children, presume that a youngster's self-concept and perception of him/herself plays a major part in his/her actions.

I submit that a fifteen year old boy who thinks of himself as a well-liked and respected student with good interpersonal skills, upon being told to do something "or else," will never, I repeat never, flash his eyes and say, "mess with me and I'll kick your butt."

The boy who says the above to his teacher, especially out loud and in front of his

friends, is the product of years and years
(fifteen to be exact) of self-concept formation
from essentially negative and destructive information.   This is a child who has been cuffed
and kicked; threatened repeatedly, and often
pointlessly punished.   This is a child who has
been neglected and shunted aside; a child for
whom excuses have been made.   Clearly in the
words of the nursery rhyme, this is "Thurs-
day's child" whose self-concept will allow him
to make the decision to be publicly defiant,
verbally abusive, physically threatening and
teacher, mom and dad, where do you think he
learned it?

    With this boy, the formula we discussed in
Chapter One, "Positive In/Positive Out," works
inside out.   "Negative In/Negative Out" very
well describes this youngster.   Remember, the
next time you are faced with unhappy confron-
tation that the child you are confronting is
merely acting out a script which has been
handed him/her for years.   You can change the
script.   You do have the power to change the
lines and affect the outcome of the play.   You
can feed a child junk food and very well expect
a sickly child: you can feed a child nutri-
tiously and very well expect a healthy youngster.   Give a kid a steady diet of specific positive encouragement and you can very well
expect a champion.

    Let's discuss how the process of positive
self-concept building works.

    Children learn our expectations of them
chiefly through what it is they do that gets
our attention.   This is what some educators who
advocate reinforcement systems like happy

faces, marbles in a jar, and M&M's do not understand about kids. The happy faces, bonus
points, marbles, tickets, etc., are a very minor
part of the reward/achievement process.

The Congressional Medal of Honor, for
example, is only a pretty ribbon and a piece of
metal, but it takes on great significance when
the President (authority symbol) presents one
to you before a joint session of Congress of the
United States. When we (authority symbols)
take our own time to stop the normal flow of
events to observe that a child has distinguished
him/herself by a particular behavior, we have
given a very special experience (lesson) to that
child. From a position of authority, we have
said "I notice you." We have said, "You are
important, special in a certain way." "You
mean something special to me." When this message of sincere emotion is plainly and obviously
tied to a specific behavior, then the likelihood
of that behavior occurring again, particularly in
our presence, is enormous. The reason is not
difficult to understand: kids, like all of us,
desire to be recognized, loved, cared for,
worried about, squeezed, hugged, helped,
praised, admired, respected, and accepted. We
all do things which we believe will earn us
these things from ourselves as well as others.
As we learn which specific behaviors earn us
these things from ourselves, as well as others,
these specific behaviors become synonymous
with the mental picture we have of who we are.
It is how we learn what makes us feel good
about ourselves.

Our job, as parents and teachers, is to
teach children and young adults how to feel
good about themselves for engaging in behavior
that will serve them well throughout their lives.

Chapter Three

DEVELOPING A POSITIVE MESSAGE SYSTEM: AN ECOLOGICAL APPROACH

There are three distinct sources of self-concept building messages in the life of a school-age child or young adult. Each of these may be considered a separate ecology. The first of these, from a teacher's standpoint, is the relationship between the teacher and the child. The quality of this relationship is largely determined by the teacher. S/he can watch for appropriate behavior and reward it or s/he can watch for inappropriate behavior and verbally or non-verbally make the child or young adult aware that s/he is acting inappropriately. Whichever the teacher chooses to spot (what is right or what is wrong) has a lot to do with how the child responds to the teacher, and it has a great deal to do with the quality of their relationship.

Adults tend to avoid other adults who offer constant criticism. The same is true of kids. However, in school, kids often have no choice. They are forced to be in a room with a teacher who is constantly critical, and compounding this negative circumstance, their self-concepts are in an extremely formative stage. Thus, a barrage of criticism may force them to retreat within themselves and form a negative picture of themselves complete with a lack of self-confidence, fear of failure, and an over-riding sense of their own short-comings. These feelings, naturally, are reflected in their behavior which tends to confirm suspicions that "they can't do it," "can't make it," and should not try. Early they come to the conclusion that someone else is the star and they are not.

One frequent response to an inundation of negative messages is defiance. Convinced that his/her role is that of "troublemaker," this powerful youngster will challenge teachers and school administrators. These kids, then, may be convinced they are a "star" of a sort. They think of themselves as skillful disruptors. Unfortunately, it not only enables them to achieve attention from parents and teachers but often earns them the adulation of their friends.

In the extreme, a defiant child develops a "get-even" outlook. This revengeful child says, in effect, "Nobody does this to me." Turning this negative self-concept into a positive one takes time, patience, understanding and all those other clichés that psychologists so often use, but to the specific, it also takes a solid control of all the ecologies (potential sources of information) in the kid's life.

Teachers who take the time to look for the strengths of a child and sincerely praise those strengths find their relationship with the student greatly strengthened, the student's performance improved, and the student's self-concept sufficiently strong to occasionally endure failure. Failure is always a learning experience to be sure, but when a student with a strong sense of who s/he is experiences failure, this student learns to correct or overcome knowing that failure is not permanent. And failure, under the supervision of a positive teacher and an encouraging parent, is how the maturation process works best. A student with a poor self-concept on the other hand, experiences failure as basically a confirmation of his/her worst suspicions about him/herself.

Within the context of what I am calling the first ecology, teachers, then, must strive to build a positive self-image in their students by

consistently rewarding appropriate behavior.
When a student feels good about him/herself,
then the first source of self-concept building
messages has done its job. A major problem
here, of course, is that teachers may be aware
of this process but they may not have received
the specific training they need to send the
quality and quantity of messages that children
and young adults need to build positive self-
images.

The second ecology or source of self-
concept building messages is the relationship
between parents and kids. Here again the
quality of this relationship is determined by the
authority figure. Parents who take little or no
interest in their offspring or who vigilantly
point to everything they do not like are sending messages that cannot possibly contribute to
a positive self-concept in their children.

Generally speaking, disinterested parents
produce reactionary children. Overly critical
parents produce insecure and tremendously
unhappy children who frequently spend their
lives in search of someone who will validate
their self-esteem. As with teachers, parents
who produce children with a positive self-
concept, with "can-do" and "go get' em" attitudes, do so by consistently praising specific
behaviors. As these children experience success and hear how important their achievements
are to the most important people in their lives,
they form a self-concept which clearly includes
all those items for which they have been
praised and from which they have experienced
the joy of achievement and success.

Of course, the same major problem for
teachers exists for parents. They have not

been trained to look for what is right in their
children, nor have they been trained to
respond appropriately when they observe these
behaviors.

The third and final source of self-concept
building messages is one which more often than
not baffles and mystifies the authority figures
in the first two ecologies. For this source, the
most powerful of all, is the child's or young
adult's peers. Very little of worth has been
written about this third ecology. Yet, in many
ways, it is the most important. When our children are small, we encourage them to develop
friendships and good social skills because as
parents and teachers we know the importance of
these skills throughout our lives. Yet in many
cases when our children pick friends and come
under their natural influence, we are frightened
or intimidated because it seems that we have no
control over the behavior of our children's
friends.

We must recognize that peer pressure,
peer approval, and the need for acceptance are
extraordinary forces in the lives of our kids.
Unfortunately, peers often encourage and
reward the wrong behavior in our children.

We also must recognize that the third ecology can be substantially controlled by parents
and teachers. Initially, parents must monitor
the influence that their children's friends have
over their own kids. Certainly this is not a
new suggestion. However, what to look for is
more important than who to look for. Parents
should realize that their children's friends (like
it or not) play a major role in building their
children's self-concepts. Parents need to ask

themselves two questions. What kind of messages are being sent to my children by their
friends? And, what kind of behavior is being
rewarded?

In other words, are my children's friends
helping to build a positive self-image for my
children or are they bossy, critical, overbear-
ing and negative? (To name just a few crip-
plers of a positive self-concept.) Or, are they
warm and encouraging and supportive of
behavior that you think is wrong for your son
or daughter. (Behaviors like using illegal
drugs, excessive alcohol, and being sexually
promiscuous.)

I want to assure you that parents do have
more control over these positive and negative
aspects of the environment than they normally
acknowledge and there are many things to say,
do, and listen for, which will be discussed in
later chapters, which can make a difference in
the quality of their children's lives and the formation of their children's self-concepts.

The same is true of teachers. Teachers
have more control over peer interaction among
their students than they often realize.
Teachers who will not tolerate students physically or psychologically abusing each other help
to create a positive environment for learning.
Gifted teachers, for example, frequently structure classroom activities so that their students
are working for a common goal or reward. As
the students participate in the achievement of a
common reward, they encourage each other to
work harder on the team. This kind of positive,
work-oriented, creative, achievement-prone
environment stimulates positive peer pressure.

In a "work for the common good" environment, a student's friends are encouraging him/her to work hard. Rewards such as extra story time, extra games, raffle prizes, etc., (for elementary age children) or reduced homework, no weekend homework, music during art class, etc. (for secondary and middle school youngsters), carry the double reinforcing effect of being a reward by the teacher or school and being greatly desired by the students as a group.

Especially skillful teachers, who have mastered the art of engineering peer teaching in their classrooms are aware that peer teaching is often as much as 30% more efficient at teaching a lesson than is the teacher alone. There are two reasons for this. Kids speak each other's "language" and few things in life are as important to a child or young adult as properly responding when his/her friend says "do it."

The total ecological approach to positive self-concept building in kids is best achieved by the close team-work of parents and teachers. At the first sign of trouble (disruption at school, defiance, refusal to do school work, homework, etc.), the parents and teachers involved must sit down and share information and together plan a strategy to help each other stop the inappropriate behavior and begin to focus specifically on the opportunities for sending the child powerful, positive messages about his/her behavior at home and/or school. In addition, both parents and teachers must discuss, openly and frankly, the specific influence the child's friends have and what steps must be taken to ensure that peer reinforcement is coming for the right reasons.

The specific skill here is the ability of
parent and teacher to communicate effectively
and not fall prey to blaming postures bringing
defenses, guilt, fear of inadequacy and other
items destructive to the specific purpose of this
critical parent/teacher meeting.

The general skill is to be positive.
Realize that each party is experiencing a certain amount of anxiety over the meeting and its
cause and quickly get to the business of how
you can work together to make sure that Sarah,
Deborah, Michael, or José is feeling good about
him/herself for coming to school on time, getting work completed, cooperating with classmates, etc. Furthermore, it is a good idea for
each of you to agree on what specific action will
be taken if the trouble continues and for both
of you to clearly communicate this message to
the kid. (The need for this type of action,
loss of privileges, time-out, detention, suspen-
sion, etc., will be reduced in direct proportion
to the success of your mutual positive plans of
action.)

PART II: THE SKILLS

"All too often a parent treats offhandedly a topic
which is crucial to his child; he does not
observe many important things that
are going on between the two
of them."

A. H. Chapman
Parents Talking, Kids Talking

"He that answereth before he heareth
showeth himself to be a fool, and
worthy of confusion."

Proverbs 18, 13

Chapter Four
POSITIVE LISTENING

Many parents and teachers don't listen! As strange as it may seem, the first important skill to master if you are going to build a positive self-concept in a young person is called positive listening. You ask, "How can something as ostensibly passive as listening help build a positive self-concept in a kid?"

This question can be answered easily when one realizes that there is nothing passive about positive listening. On the contrary, positive listening is actively observing all the positive aspects of what our kids say and do. By "listening" I mean using all our senses to collect as much information as we can about our children and students. This includes what we hear with our ears, see with our eyes, smell (what is that funny smoke?) with our noses, and intuit with that parent/teacher sixth sense that we all seem to have.

Lets look at an example of a parent who doesn't listen:

Parent: Oh, you are wearing your new tennies (Van's, Off-The-Wall, special slip-on super grip deck shoes – $23.95 at this writing).

Son: Aren't they hot? I just love them.

Parent: Do they fit?

Son: These are such a super birthday gift. Thank you very much.

Parent: You're welcome. I'm glad you like them.

Son: These are so hot! (Hint: "hot"
                means very socially acceptable.)
                They are the thing to have at
                school. And, speaking of
                school, I'm going to be late.
                Catch you later.

Because the parent in the above dialogue
lacked "active listening" skills (the new buzz
word in communication training), the parent
missed the fact that s/he did not get an answer
to a very critical question, "Do they fit?" As
all parents of thirteen year-olds will tell you,
the fit of the shoe is a critical item because a
too snug fit today means another $23.95 tomor-
row.

Advocates of "active listening" skills will
say that with practice (and bitter experience!),
it is easy and rewarding to actively participate
in conversations with children – to listen for
what they do not say or do not answer in order
to learn to better communicate with them.

So consider the same situation with a
parent who is an "active listener" – a real
Sherlock Holmes.

Parent: Oh, you are wearing your new
                tennies!

Son: Aren't they hot? I just love
                them.

Parent: Do they fit?

Son: These are such a super birthday
                gift. Thank you very much.

Parent: You're welcome. But do they fit?

Son: These are so hot!

Parent: David, you did not answer my
           question. Why are you avoiding
           my question?

Son: (With slight coloration of guilt
           and protesting.) They fit fine.

Parent: Let me feel your toe. (Does so.)
           Your toe is up to here. These
           don't fit. They will be too small
           in a week! And you knew it.
           You were not going to say a
           word just so you could wear
           them today, and lie. Sit there
           and lie through your teeth! (So
           much for a happy birthday.)

I will spare you the rest of the dialogue
since I suspect you have seen this play
before – another time, another theatre.

My point is simple: "active" listening is
not enough – although it is a step in the right
direction. Most parents and teachers, pre-
occupied with worries, concerns, the needs of
their own lives and the needs of other kids,
rarely actively listen. When they do, so often
the results are negative, because like some
super sleuth, they are constantly in an adver-
sarial role with kids – alert always to what
they are "up to." As in "what are those little
devils up to now?"

The skill of positive listening is comprised
of two parts. First, active listening and close

observation. Second, rigorously seeking the
positive values of any given situation to make
that experience a positive learning experience
for a kid.

Consider the scene one more time.

Parent: Oh, you are wearing your new
          tennies!

Son: Aren't they hot? I just love
          them.

Parent: Do they fit?

Son: These are such a super birthday
          gift. Thank you very much.

Parent: You're welcome. But do they
          fit?

Son: These are so hot!

Parent: (Skill one; part one.) David,
          do your tennis shoes fit?

Son: (With slight coloration of guilt
          and protesting.) They fit fine.

Parent: Let me feel your toe. (Does so.)
          These don't fit. They will be
          too small in a week. I under-
          stand the situation. You wanted
          to wear your new tennis shoes to
          school on your birthday. The
          thought of wearing your old ones
          was unattractive. If you wear
          them today and they get dirty –
          which they will – we cannot

return and exchange them. In a
few weeks, they will cramp and
hurt your feet. You will not
want to wear them. We will all
be very upset. (Spells out
natural consequences.) What do
you think we should do?

Son: (Disappointed and facing reality.)
            We'll take them back and get a
            half-size larger. I will wear my
            old ones today. (Kids can
            handle disappointment – they
            can!)

If at this point the parent has been looking for the positive potentials for learning in
this situation, s/he should have determined that
there is substantial opportunity to teach his/her
son the value of family cooperation, that waiting
to get things right is preferable to hurrying
and getting things wrong, that he can survive
disappointment, and that he is a responsible
member of the family. When a parent detects
these kinds of opportunities, s/he is a positive
listener.

When these opportunities are realized
through "positive talking" (discussed in the
next chapter), then parents are on their way to
building positive self-concepts in their kids.

Consider what happens to David: instead
of looking down at new shoes all day and feeling the pain of guilt, knowing that the day of
reckoning is not far away, David looked down
at his disgraceful, old shoes all day and feels

good about himself. He is a good person, he
thinks as he looks down – "I can handle these
shoes one more day." In fact, he's proud of
these shoes, for now they carry a special meaning. They are a visable reminder of his sense
of responsibility, and that he is a good family
member.

Now, the "jaundiced eye" is blinking once
again: But the kid lied! He lied! What are
you going to do about that? Well, the truth
is, he didn't lie, actually. David said, "They
fit fine." And they did. But not the right
"fine."

But, if this kind of "truth coloration" or
bending or shaping of the facts is leading to a
serious problem – that is, overt and frequent
lying, then you can, and should do something
about it. You could tell him, calmly, that his
lying cost him the use of his bicycle for a
week, or some other appropriate deprivation.
But you don't yell, scream, shout, threaten or
otherwise remonstrate unless you wish to send
many negative messages, which, I promise, will
soon come back to you.

The point is that a kid who learns to
accept disappointment and accept responsibility
will not only feel good about him/herself, but
this kid will have no need to lie the next time a
similar situation arises.

Just think of the few extra minutes it
takes to look for positive values in our
children. Compare this to a lifetime of misery,
worry, and unhappiness caused by a kid with
low self-esteem and a negative self-concept. As

a teacher and counselor, I have said to so many
parents who cannot take the time to be positive, "Mr. and Mrs. Whitman, we have David
this year and next; you have him forever!"

Now, let's look at a typical school situation
for another example of positive listening in
action. (A private conversation.)

Student: Mrs. Jenkins?

Teacher: Yes, what is it, Stuart?

Student: I can't do this stuff, today.

Teacher: Why?

Student: I'm very upset, today. My parents had a big fight last night
and I couldn't sleep. My dad,
he left last night, slammed the
door. I'm really upset bad.

Teacher: Well, it will blow over. It always
does. If you don't feel well
today, just sit quietly and don't
bother anyone else.

This is a classic case of not listening to
the message. A close look at Stuart's eyes
would confirm his lack of sleep. A close look
at his pupils might disclose something about
drug involvement – a sniff of his breath may
disclose something about his involvement with
alcohol. But these things, along with the pain-
ful story, are unpleasant and the easiest thing
for the teacher to do is say "just don't bother
anyone else today."

The same situation with an "active listener" teacher might indeed disclose something
of the truth, of drugs or booze, or a simpler
truth, his parents did collide last night. The
active listener without the positive skills might
say, "Parents had a fight, right – about you on
drugs. I'm a teacher with a room full of dilated
pupils, and you have two of them!"

The positive listener, however, would
detect the most significant message; s/he would
read Stuart's verbal and non-verbal behavior as
a plea for help – especially at a time when his
security at home has been shaken. The last
response a kid needs whose family life has been
disrupted is a weak and non-supportive "do
what you want" from his teacher.

There are (of course) many avenues for
teachers to take with students like Stuart.
Parent involvement, support from the administration, help from a social worker, training
about drug abuse from local law enforcement
personnel, etc. But the success of those inter-
ventions all depend on Stuart recognizing that
his teacher is not the enemy. Teachers and
parents must master the art of positive listening
to avoid becoming the enemy. Fortunately, the
various subskills of positive listening are easy
to learn and yield wonderful results.

One.   Give the kid your complete attention.
          Sometimes your complete attention
          alone is all that the situation requires.
          Note of warning: If your complete
          attention is impossible at the time,
          i.e., you are busy with another
          youngster or you are in the middle of

a lesson, make a specific time available when you can give your complete attention and <u>don't</u> <u>break</u> <u>the</u> <u>date</u>.

Two. Analyze the <u>kid's</u> <u>non-verbal</u> <u>language</u>. While it is very important to listen to his/her words, remember up to 80% of what s/he is saying is being non-verbally communicated. Look for signs that conflict: often kids will say one thing with their mouths and say the opposite with their bodies. Example: to a direct question while saying "Yes" s/he will shake his/her head "No." If you are worried about the truth, look into his/her eyes. Remember, anyone can lie, but it takes a master – bordering on the pathological – to lie with his/her eyes. And, look for eye contact.* A lack of eye contact, especially during normal, non-threatening conversations, may be one significant sign of a reduced self-concept.

Three. Don't <u>make</u> <u>snap</u> <u>judgments</u>. Listen, observe, and, above all else, stay calm. Hysteria only complicates the healing process and, worse, stupid and sometime vicious things are said in anger and they can <u>never</u> be retracted. Stay cool mom <u>and</u> dad; stay relaxed, teacher. Children and young adults do not respect people who are always coming unhinged.

*There are cultural variations in eye contact behavior that may need to be considered with ethnic minority children.

Four. Listen for what is avoided. Children
and young adults with a negative
self-concept will invariably diminish
their positive contributions to a particular situation. By recognizing and
observing their particular worth and
by pointing out to them what they did
that was useful, intelligent, caring,
etc., you do two wonderful things;
1) you show them their worth in your
eyes and 2) you teach them to look
for the positive aspects of problem
situations.

Five. Overcome your impulse to talk. This
may be the toughest subskill to master in positive listening. As parents
and teachers we are programmed to
spew information as soon as a kid
moves into range. You cannot be a
positive listener and talk at the same
time.

Six. Be vigilant for the positive aspects of
the situation. Virtually all situations
have their positive aspects. Of
course, this excludes the heinous:
("Didn't that gun make a surprisingly
loud noise when you pulled the
trigger!")

By looking for what is right about a kid,
we have the raw materials to begin the self-
concept building process. Positive self-concepts
take time, energy, patience, and love to build.
They can be damaged in a split second. When
our positive listening yields good things about a
kid, we can use those good things to begin a
series of positive messages which will aid the

healing process and start the kid on the road
to thinking of him/herself as a champion. And
teacher, mom and dad, like the cereal ad told
us so many times when we were kids ourselves, "champions are made, not born."

Chapter Five
POSITIVE TALKING

Once positive listening has yielded a place to start, then it is time to make a positive response. Unfortunately and for a lot of reasons, many parents and teachers are seriously deficient in this critical skill. Certainly few parents and, surprisingly few teachers have been trained in the use of effective positive reinforcement. Those who have received some kind of "behavior modification" training often fail to realize (maybe because of a shaky self-concept themselves), how supremely important their emotional responses are to kids. Kids want to know we feel good about them. They constantly study us watching for signs of approval. Winks, smiles, warm hellos, pats, hugs, playful teasing, joking, and sharing "secrets" are all part of the interpersonal intimacies of acceptance and love that kids crave. They want to share their lives with us and their feelings with us. They want so much to be accepted and not condoned, proud and not embarrassed, victorious and not defeated.

Talking positive is the way to begin to reach out and connect with kids whose self-concepts need help. But first, for the purposes of contrast, let's consider the following negative situations:

Student: Does this mean I scored the highest grade in the class?

Teacher: Don't let it go to your head.

* * *

Son: Hey, sports fans, look at this report card. Four "A's" and a "B."

Dad: "B"?   What   did   you   get   a   "B"
       in?

* * *

Daughter: My face is looking so much bet-
          ter since I changed medication.

Mother: Just don't forget to use it or
         you'll look like a pizza again.

Many times kids hide their need for approval and support behind a mask of bravado.
Parents and teachers, who are not positive
listeners, may feel a need to "take them down a
notch or two" out of some unfounded and
foolish fear that they will "get too big for their
britches." Parents and teachers frequently
respond to those plain messages for approval
with disapproval – at times laced with sarcasm
or even bitter rancor.

What does the father who responds to his
son's nearly perfect report card hope to
accomplish by commenting on its sole imperfec-
tion? If he thinks his reaction will motivate his
son to greater achievement, he is unwise.
Achievement is born of self-worth. When it is
accompanied by a desire to sting, put down, or
"show somebody a thing or two," it has very
nasty side-effects. Champions who use their
power for revenge can be very unpleasant to
live with.

When rancor motivates a parental response,
nothing but trouble results. A mother who
responds to her daughter's thinly-disguised
request for encouragement about her improved
acne condition with a scournful reminder and
an insensitive simile can hardly expect her

daughter to seek her counsel and support when
she is in serious trouble.

Most unforgivable is a teacher, one of
whose primary mission is to build confidence in
kids, verbally slapping down a child who is
really asking "Didn't I do well? Aren't you
pleased with me?" Many teachers say such
things as "Don't let it go to your head" because
such one liners entertain the class. This enter-
tainment is costly, indeed. For a student who
is derided by peers because of a witty Groucho
Marx or Don Rickles line by the teacher has
learned a terrible thing – that for the sake of
a laugh, or the sense of power or control, the
teacher would hurt him/her. Such teachers
may have the air let out of their tires or
"super glue" squirted into their car door locks.
And it isn't because they are loved and
respected.

Contrast this to the teacher who has positive listening and responding skills. Let's consider the first situation again.

Student: Does this mean I scored the
highest grade in the class?

Teacher: Yes it does. Your hard work
has paid off handsomely. It is
an impressive achievement.

Because this teacher positively listened
and heard the "notice me" in the student's
question, and because this teacher realized that
a positive response – sincerely delivered – was
a golden opportunity (an "I like what you
did"), we can all safely bet that we will see
hard work from this student in the future. If

a sufficient amount (and this amount varies from kid to kid) of positive response about hard work and academic achievement comes from all the significant others in this kid's life, s/he will form a positive self-concept which includes hard work and academic achievement. Once this concept is formed, then the true reward for hard work and academic achievement comes from within.

Consider the second situation.

Son: Hey sports fans, look at this report card. Four "A's" and a "B".

Father: Hey! Fabulous. That's Honor Roll. Paul, this means the Honor Roll! You are looking at one proud father! Wait 'til your mother sees this!

Here the father expends no more energy than in our first example. Yet, because of his words, and because of his body language which is beaming with pride, his son has felt a totally different response. His son feels that jolt of kinesthetic energy which accompanies great achievement – the same energy he would feel if he hit the ball out of the park to win the game and as he rounded third base, saw his father jumping up and down in the stands hugging his mother.

Well, dad, four "A's" and a "B" means that kid has just cleared the bases in the game of life, and if you miss the fact that your son has just won the game, and worse, you say "You call that a home run? It barely squeeked

over the fence," you are well on your way to
striking out in your own game of life. Remember when its late in your own game and you are
many runs behind – he lives in another city,
hasn't called for months, has been in and out
of trouble with the law, can't seem to keep a
steady job – remember how you left so many
runners stranded on base in the early innings
of the game – remember how your runner got
thrown out because you sent him the wrong
signal.

Now, let's examine the third situation.

Daughter: My face is looking so much better since I changed the medication.

Mother: You deserve the credit for that.
You haven't missed a day. That
kind of dedication pays off. I
am thrilled for you.

Here again is a mother who has detected
that her teenage daughter is saying "I'm here,
too. I'm doing my best. Right? Isn't that
right?" Mother catches an opportunity to
reinforce the kind of dedication she has
observed in her daughter. Her response is a
simple, but very powerful, "I like you." It has
greater value than a new dress (as a reward)
for the prom, or a new car, a blank check, or
a "shared" master charge (she gets the card/
you get the bill).

The feeling of happiness (felt in a sincere
response), with no reservation, strings, condi-
tionals, or other items to diminish the excitement of the moment has a power to do what

material items can only symbolize. Material
items can never substitute for you.

A parent or teacher who is a positive
talker seeks always to make a positive, self-
concept building response to kids. Of course,
this is easy to say and, at times, extremely
difficult to do. You will master the art of
positive talking if you practice the following
subskills of the positive response.

One.   Make your body send the same mes-
         age your mouth is sending. A kid
         who is looking into armor-piercing
         eyes and hearing words chattering
         like a machine gun through clenched
         teeth may miss the meaning of "You
         are doing good work today."

Two.   Avoid using sarcasm. Parents and
         teachers whose habit it is to deliver a
         message with two meanings often draw
         "Do you really mean it?" looks when
         they sincerely praise kids. If you
         must be sarcastic, confine your
         remarks to the subject matter. Never
         be sarcastic about kids – never.
         Parents who use sarcasm to control
         children should be advised that they
         will be controlled by the same weapon
         when they are the kids and their kids
         are their parents. Nursing home con-
         versations are incredibly revealing
         about the past.

Three.   Put some emotion in your positive
         response. Let them know you mean
         it. Remember champions thrive on
         the applause and adulation of the

crowd. Even if you know in your
heart you are the best and have the
most solid positive self-concept in the
world, there is nothing like being
called from the dugout by a standing
ovation. Nothing like the roses hitting
the stage to cries of "encore!"
Nothing like being carried from the
field on the shoulders of your team-
mates to the deafening roar of the
crowd. Nothing like reading the tele-
gram congratulating you on a Pulitzer
Prize. These are the magic moments
of life. How is a kid going to
develop a taste of victory, unless we,
who are the first audience, give him/
her a sample of the sweetness of
victory? The more you yell and
scream about something good the less
you will have cause to yell and
scream about something bad. Note of
warning: Don't be phony. If yelling
and screaming about something good
isn't your style, don't do it. But do
something to let that kid know you
think s/he is a star, or s/he may
never be one. And if you ever think
that not all of us can be stars, spend
a few days in a rehabilitation ward
for disabled children. Watch a child
with no arms feed herself with her
feet and then tell me some of us cannot be stars!

Four. Single out specific behaviors for
praise. Tie your positive response to
specific behaviors which you want to
see in the future. Kids love to find
out what it is we expect of them.

This gives them a way to get our
attention for beneficial rather than
destructive activities. The general
praise ("I like you") is worthwhile,
but it can lose impact quickly. ("I
know. I know. You like me
already.") Specific praise such as
"Jan, when I pass your room and it
looks as neat as the Hilton, I feel like
I'm doing a good job at being a
parent. Thank you." is much more
effective because the next time Jan
feels a need for a positive response
from you, she will clean and straigh-
ten her room. Note of warning: Do
not fall into the trap of "please,
please me or else." Parents who
make their affection and positive
responses conditional ("If you are
home on time, I will love you; if you
are not, I will not speak to you for a
week") are playing a dangerous game
called "power struggle." In this
game someone always loses and in
parent-child and teacher-student relationships, when one party wins at the
other party's expense, both parties
lose. The "please, please me or else"
trap is easily avoided. Sample:
"Maria you look stunning. You
should have a smashing time tonight!
By the way, I expect you home no
later than 12:30. If you are going to
be a little late, don't have Dennis
drive wrecklessly, call and explain.
If you do not call and you are not
home by 12:30, you are grounded for
two weeks by your own choice. Now,
have a great time. I love you."

Five.   Once is never enough. Just because
you made a big fuss over the fact
that he went to the potty all by himself yesterday is no reason not to
make a big fuss today. It will only
lose its meaning if you don't mean it.
One father I know has a wonderful
solution to the problem of sending
repeated positive messages. He would
say, after his oldest son had done
something particularly unselfish,
"You're making points, Mark, you're
making points." His son told me it
wasn't long before he realized that
the points were not being tallied and
there was no prize waiting at the
end. What he discovered was that
"you're making points" was his
father's sincere way of telling him, an
athlete, that he was winning the
game. Furthermore, the son knew
that by being unselfish or by giving
freely of his time and effort for the
betterment of others, he would
undoubtedly attract his father's
attention. When you are the oldest of
five children, positive parental attention can be a rare item, and from
his father's point of view, having five
children is a lot easier when the
eldest is "unselfish" and helpful.

Six.   Never give up. The positive effects
of your effort to build a positive self-
concept in a kid may not be immediately apparent. (Here's a scary
thought: the negative effects of your
negative and punishing responses are
not always immediately apparent,

either! Parents and teachers who
insist on using corporal punishment,
and who defensively point to its
effectiveness are short-sighted.
While "paddling" a youngster may
very well get him to behave, it also
teaches that physical violence is an
appropriate response when someone
does not do what you tell him/her to
do. Makes you wonder why we live
in such a violent country, doesn't
it?)

Keep at it. There is a positive value
and something to be learned by every
situation. Oddly enough, this skill of
positive persistence is one that many
teachers lack. We tend to try something once or twice and then dismiss
it if we see no immediate reaction.
Remember the sage advice of the
English poet, Geoffrey Chaucer:
"Life is so short and the craft is so
long to learn."

To sum up, the skill of positive talking
accomplishes a number of important tasks in the
process of building a positive self-concept in
kids. In the first place, it lets the kids know
you like them. Secondly, it helps to communicate your high expectations for them. Third, it
teaches kids to be positive in their approach to
their own problems. Fourth, it sets a positive
tone to your relationships and keeps those lines
of communication. Finally, a positive response
is the best defense against the biggest psychological crippler of all kids – "I can't." Motivation is born of a will to do and do well. Champions always say, "Put me in, coach. Just get

---

me on that field. Oh, come on coach, let me at
'em."

    If you have done your job well, mom and
dad, and if you have consistently responded in
a positive and reinforcing way, teacher, there
is no feeling which can match the one you get
when they ask for the chance to try something
new and you say, "GO GET 'EM!"

PART III.   PRACTICE

*"It is better to be invited to herbs with
love than to a fatted calf with hatred."*

Proverbs 15, 17

*"Developing respect for the parents is the
critical factor in child management."*

Dr. James Dobson
Dare To Discipline

*"In the morning sow thy seed, and in the
evening let not thy hand cease, for thou
knowest not which may spring up, this
or that; and if both together, it
shall be the better."*

Ecclesiastes 11, 6

Chapter Six
TIPS FOR PARENTS IN TROUBLE

Practicing the skills of positive listening and positive talking will yield good results for parents who have previously established positive communication patterns with their children. But what about these skills and their effectiveness when the parent-child relationship is shakey or has gone sour? How can a parent in trouble build a positive self-concept in a kid when their history has been a solid stream of negative information about each other?

Here are four tips for parents in trouble. By following the suggestions in the tips, studying the illustrations, and completing the exercises, you will begin to practice the principles on which this book is based. Note of warning: You must believe in yourself and believe you have the power to change the kind and quality of messages you are sending your youngster. If you do not believe you can change you are wasting your time reading this book. If you believe you cannot change yourself, how can you possibly change a kid? It is so much easier to raise winners when you act like a winner yourself.

Tip One: Take Honest Stock of Yourself.

Sit down in a quiet, reflective moment and take a brutally honest look at who you are, what you believe in, and what you do to support or supplant those beliefs. Are you a "do as I say, not as I do" parent? Do you rant on a soapbox about drugs to your kids and then down three martinis at the end of the day? Do you get upset when your kids are suspended from school for smoking when you are still on two packs a day? Do you worry about what foods your children are eating when you are carrying thirty pounds more than you should and never watch TV without "munchies"? Do you want loving, long-lasting, and wonderfully reinforcing relationships for your children someday, when you are "in the process" of divorce number four?

These are tough questions, mom and dad, but they must be asked not by me, but by you of yourself. Because it is very hard to help your children decide what is "right" for them, if it is obvious to them that you do not know what is "right" for you. If you are like the rest of us, your self-assessment will turn up a number of areas in your personal life which need attention. And, you cannot fix them all overnight. So, pick out one, one that is fixable, and work on it. Furthermore, let everybody in the family know you are working on it. They will help support you as you change. Now, instead of telling your kids how to live their lives, you are showing them – modeling for them – how an adult tackles a tough problem and wins.

Illustration For Tip One

Steven, a 17 year-old high school drop-out and his father, Peter Smith, an insurance executive, had a terrible and hateful relationship. Peter on Steven: "Kid is into drugs. Nothing heavy, mostly marijuana, has a girl and he spends all his time at her place. Dropped out of high school – even though he had good grades. When he smart mouthed me, I used to work him over good, but now he's bigger than I am and about a year ago he really cleaned my clock. Can't wait until he's eighteen and I can throw him out. A damn shame you know, kid is awfully bright." Steven on Peter: "He comes home, has a few drinks, and first thing you know he's on my case. Usually it's, well, if you're not in school, then get a job. You think I want to end up like him? Fat, over forty, and stuck on a treadmill kissing up to somebody all day? Don't get me wrong, my dad's not a bad guy, he's just a jerk sometimes."

It was clear that both father and son wanted their relationship to be different but neither knew where to begin. When Peter took a good look at himself, he realized that he hadn't set a very good example for Steven to follow. So the first thing he did was cut out hard alcohol. The second thing he did, at my suggestion, was to start a light jogging and exercise program before work everyday. After nearly a month, he had lost nine pounds and told me he never felt better in his life. I suggested he invite Steven to run with him in the mornings after making a pact with Steven that during workouts they would send no negative messages to each other. Steven told me later

that those first couple of days were awfully
quiet mornings, but later they talked about
"safe" subjects like the weather and the morning air. Peter told me privately that he almost
fell over the day Steven told him, "You run
pretty well for an old guy." Ultimately Steven
finished a GED (high school equivalency
diploma) and went to college.

Exercise For Tip One

Complete the following self-assessment. It will give you insight into your own self-concept. Score 10 points for a "yes" answer, 5 points for a "sometimes" answer, and 0 for a "no."

Score 100	you're lying
75-95	you're okay
50-70	shakey
below 50	get your act together

1. Do I live by an established and consistent set of rules?

    _____

2. Do I periodically revise my set of rules when it is prudent and appropriate to do so?

    _____

3. Do I refuse to force my values and standards for my own life on other members of my family?

    _____

4. Do I look at both sides of an issue, and do I look at positive outcomes for each course of action?

    _____

5. Can I control my anger and do I have the strength to restrain rage?

    _____

6. Do I respond positively to genuine and well-intended criticism?

    _____

7.   Can I accept lifestyles which are different
     from my own?

                                        _____

8.   Do I look for positive value in other
     people's solutions to problems we have in
     common?

                                        _____

9.   Do I ask the same behavior of my children
     that I expect from myself?

                                        _____

10. Do I stay cool under fire when I am chal-
     lenged by my children?

                                        _____

     A final comment about Tip One: Taking
Honest Stock of Yourself. If your current
score shows need for improvement, pick an area
and go to work. Then re-do the above
exercise in three months. If by that time your
score has improved, and you have been honest,
then I guarantee your relationship with your
kids has improved. For those of you who have
trouble with self-deception, ask another member
of your family to "check" your answers. You
may be astonished at the results.

Tip Two: <u>Learn to Accept What You Cannot Change and Look for Positive
Value in it.</u>

　　If you have made a decision to raise children as a divorced single parent, then live with
that decision and do not be wracked with guilt
every time the kids do something you don't like.
That guilt and the compensations you make
because of it will begin to show in your relationship with your kids. Learning to accept
what you can't change is an important step
toward feeling good about yourself as a person.
It is difficult to act like a champion when you
feel guilty about something you have done.
When you are crippled with self-doubt about a
course of action, you will send conflicting and
inconsistent messages to your kids. It is very
hard to look for positive values in your youngsters when you are unhappy yourself.

Illustration For Tip Two

Tanya, age 15, finally told her parents that she was pregnant. She refused to disclose the father, partly because of fear of what her father might do to the boy and partly because she wasn't sure which one of three possible boys was the father. Her mother was very helpful. All she did was cry.

When Tanya would come into the room, her mother would start to cry. When she did say anything, she said, through tears, "How could you do this to us?" and "What did we do to deserve this?" Tanya's father was even more helpful. He referred to Tanya's unborn baby as "the little bastard" and to Tanya as a "slut." It isn't a great wonder why Tanya got herself in this mess in the first place. Clearly, her self-concept was in such bad shape from the negative messages her parents had been sending her over the years that she found herself in the comforting arms of the first three boys who paid her any positive attention. Sexual promiscuity and a diminished self-concept are old friends.

The thing to be learned here is what's done is done, and Tanya's parents must accept it. To further send negative messages will not solve this problem or make the baby go away. The healing and building process must begin, and there is much work to be done. The sad aspect of this case is that since Tanya's parents focused on everything she did that was wrong and failed to build her self-concept, Tanya, working from her parents as a model, will begin to send the same kind of self-concept destroying messages to her child. Can't you

imagine the love and attention "the little bastard" will get at home? It will not be many
years before he lives up to his name.

Exercise For Tip Two

I.   Down the left-hand side of a sheet of paper, make a list of all the things your children do that you do not like. Down the right-hand side, make a list of all the things they do that you like.

Example

Marla: Age 9

Dislike	Like
(1) Watches TV too much.	(1) Goes to bed on time.
(2) Waits to the last minute to do her homework.	(2) Is courteous; says please and thank you.
(3) Does not hang her clothes in the closet.	(3) Has good telephone manners.
(4) Hates to visit with her father – fights with her stepbrother. Gets scolded by her stepmother.	(4) Has good eyecontact when meeting new people.
(5) Hates to wear her orthodonture retainer.	

II.   Now think back to how long it took you to write each side of the list. If you are like most parents, you did the left side in seconds; the right side took longer, and

you had to think about it. Tells you
something, doesn't it?

III. Look down the right-hand column (things
you like) and ask yourself this tough
question: How many times, last week, did
I praise him/her for one or more of the
above? If your answer is at least once
per item, congratulate yourself on doing a
good job building a positive self-concept in
your kid. If it isn't at least once, then
get to work.

IV. Look down the left-hand column (things
you don't like) and ask yourself this tough
question: How many times last week did
we discuss; I yell and scream about; I
lose my temper about; I spend hours on
the phone talking to my analyst, ex-
husband, or my own mother about? Very
revealing, isn't it? Do you see how Marla
has learned to get your attention?

V. Once more look down the left hand column
(dislike). Which of the five behaviors
are you least likely to change and have
little or (in some cases) no control over?
I hope you said, "Number four, hates to
visit her father, etc." If you did, you
are mastering the point of Tip Two:
Learn to Accept What You Can't Change.
So, look for the positive (skill one) and
respond positively (skill two): "Marla,
your father has a right, by nature and
by civil law, to see you and spend time
with you. And he loves you! Life will
confront you with difficult people, and you
must develop skills to cope with them. So
learning to cope with your brother,

Marvin, and your father's wife, whom your father loves very much, is great practice for you in the future. I know you are strong and can handle this situation well. I love you, too!"

Tip Three:	Establish Reasonable and Serious Rules For Your Household and Catch the Kids Following the Rules

All effective management systems begin with the rules. The rules for the household are the official by-laws by which all members of the household live. Rules of the house are clearly communicated expectations of behavior for all. These rules should be worded very clearly, or the power children in your family will play "lawyer" with you. Example: instead of "no rough-housing" or "no horseplay" – both of which are metaphorical in nature – get specific. Example: "no pushing, shoving, kicking, hitting, spitting, or biting, ever." Here are some more examples for specific household rules which families have found useful:

1. All beds made in the morning by the persons who slept in them.

2. All dirty laundry will be deposited in the dirty clothes hamper by the person who wore it last.

3. All lights will be turned off by the person who leaves the room last.

4. The garage door stays closed at all times except when in use.

5. First task of the morning. Brush your teeth.

6. Rubber band retainers for orthodonture appliances found on the floor, floating in the soup, stuck against

the ceiling, etc. will cost you $1.00 apiece. Money will automatically be deducted from your savings account, including birthday money.

7. No one leaves this house without letting someone know, in person, by phone, or by note, 1) where s/he is going to be, and 2) when s/he will return, and, if possible, a phone number where we can reach you.

8. Bedrooms will be dusted, straightened, and swept at least once per week by the person(s) who sleep in them.

9. All homework will be completed by no later than the night before it is due.

10. All homework will be checked and signed by a parent before it is turned in.

11. All arguments will be settled by the persons involved, peaceably, unless a house rule has been broken. Then we want to know about it.

12. All prescriptions and other internal medication is in one place, (medicine cabinet) which is always locked, and mother has the only key.

13. Kids can consume alcoholic beverages only in the presence of a parent.

14. Any trouble at school – including being warned or disciplined by a

teacher or administrator – will be
reported to mom or dad the night of
the day it happened. No exceptions.

15. No one is to take illicit drugs, smoke
    or eat marijuana; sniff, snort, or
    inject mind-altering substances; or
    engage in any activity they would not
    do in front of mom and dad.

16. Fire: Get everybody out –
                   take no personal pro-
                   perty. Call the fire
                   department.

    Tornado: Go to the basement.

    Earthquake: Climb under a table
                   or stand in a doorway;
                   after the shaking, go
                   to the middle of the
                   baseball field across
                   the street. Wait 'til
                   we get there.

17. No one says or does anything to any-
    one which could possibly hurt his/her
    feelings.

18. No derogatory nicknames such as:
    "metal mouth," "elephant breath,"
    "bird brain," "Dolly Parton," etc.)

19. If you can't say something nice or
    constructive about or to someone,
    don't say it.

20. Telephones will be answered "(family
    name)" residence. This is "your
    name". To take a message, make a

note of the call, including the time, and leave it by the phone in the kitchen.

21. The person eating or drinking the last of an item will automatically record that item on the kitchen shopping list.

22. No offensive language in this house.

23. No teasing which results in hurt feelings or tears.

24. All pets will be cared for – cages cleaned, fed, watered, bathed, deflead, etc. by their owners and <u>no one else</u>.

25. No loud music after 9:30 PM.

26. All new friends will spend <u>at least</u> one evening at the house get<u>ting to</u> know us. <u>We want to know your friends</u>.

27. Be polite. No vulgar animal noises in this house.

28. Do not wash your hair in the sink. Wash the sink after you use it.

29. No running or ball playing in the house.

30. Do not drink soda pop with sugar in it or eat "junk food" with additives, preservatives, or food dyes in them.

Exercise For Tip Three

I.   By yourself or with your spouse, and
     using the above list as inspiration only,
     construct your own list of house rules
     using this guideline: keep the list to the
     absolute minimum number needed to run
     your household. Too many rules are as
     bad as too few.

II. Sit down, at a quiet and appropriate time,
     communicate and discuss the rules with
     your kids. Answer all questions, clarify
     all rules with concrete examples, change
     any rules which are unclear or fail to com-
     municate your intent.

III. Explain what will happen when house rules
     are broken. (Hint: you'd better do some-
     thing every time the rules are broken, or
     they will think you don't care about the
     rules you made.)

IV. Tell them what will result if they follow
     the rules. This is the most important
     aspect of your communication. All must
     understand that very positive and good
     things will happen as a result of all follow-
     ing the rules. Coaches, who are all firm
     believers in training rules (ask one, if you
     don't believe me), point out frequently to
     their teams that by following training rules
     the team will develop team spirit, cohesive-
     ness, a sense of unity and purpose, a
     winning attitude, and a strong sense of
     identity — in short, mom and dad, every-
     thing you want for your family.

V.   In the first few weeks after you have
      instituted your rules, vigilantly exercise
      the skills of positive listening and positive
      talking. By stating the rules, you have
      set up the perfect opportunity to practice
      your new skills of watching for opportun-
      ities to build the self-concept of your chil-
      dren. Positive self-concepts are built
      because kids feel good about themselves
      for accepting the responsibility for their
      own behavior. You can start this process
      of accepting responsibility by 1) giving
      them rules to live by and 2) pointing out
      how well they are doing. If that sounds
      like an oversimplification, it isn't. You
      don't have to be a genius or a behavioral
      scientist to raise champions. You must,
      however, follow learning theorist Wesley
      Becker's most famous directive on kids:

      "Catch them being good."

      By setting rules, you are creating natural
      opportunities to follow this man's excellent
      advice.

VI.   Periodically, revise your rules and let
      everyone know you have done so. As
      your kids grow, your household will auto-
      matically change. If you have done a good
      job at self-concept building in their early
      years, their later years will be a pleasure.
      But never believe that any of us are so
      mature and responsible that we can live
      without rules. (Maturity means living by
      a set of rules.) Rules, particularly ones
      made by an individual for him/herself, are
      the quintessential benchmarks of self-
      discipline. One other point: never forget

that kids crave discipline. This is why they will always make tougher rules for their own behavior than we would for them. What better way to say, "I love you," than to say, "I noticed you made your bed. Nice job, Roger. Good going."

Tip Four: Whatever Happens, Keep Talking
                  and Don't Give Up.

Ridiculous postures like "Go and never darken our door again" or turning the kid's picture to the wall only serve to hurt and continue to send the negative messages that ruined your relationship in the first place. Thunderous pronouncements of doom and having the lawyers revise the will are always regretted later. Keep those lines of communication open because when kids can't turn to their parents, they turn to someone else. This certainly should explain the astounding number of teenage runaways and the phenomenon of the quasireligious cults overflowing with young people prepared to adorn themselves in unfamiliar garb and engage in strange and nonsensical behaviors. Everyone needs someone to talk to, mom and dad; if things are very, very bad, do something intelligent and seek professional help. You wouldn't think of treating an inflamed appendix by yourself; a serious rupture in the family lines of communication can be as deadly as peritonitis. It is a very hard thing to say to you, but parents who bury their overdosed children always say, "If only s/he had come to me. I didn't realize. My God, I didn't realize."

Ask friends whose judgments you trust for a recommendation; you will be surprised how many of them sought professional help and received excellent care and valuable, practical advice. If you do not want to ask friends, pick up the yellow pages and look under "marriage and family counselors." Pick out a name, make an appointment, and go. If you don't like that person, pick out another name until you find someone you like, trust, and who can help you re-establish basic communication with your kid. You cannot help build a self-concept if you are not talking.

Illustration For Tip Four

Delia Paterson was told by the teachers and the school psychologist that her 12 year-old, Delvin, was exhibiting symptoms of "the hyperkinetic syndrome." She had to admit it: Delvin couldn't sit still for ten seconds. She had tried beating him; threatening him; depriving him of television, his bicycle, and his skateboard. He would not sit down and do his homework. Then he started running away from home. Once, he covered twenty miles before a squad car picked him up because they didn't recognize him from their neighborhood. The school psychologist recommended that Delia have Delvin "looked at" by the local pediatrician, who promptly prescribed Ritalin. That certainly stopped the running away. Delvin didn't have the energy to push a pencil. This solution sure made his teachers happy. When Delvin arrived at school, the first thing they asked him was "Did you take your medication today?"

The only person who wasn't happy was Delia Paterson. She noticed Delvin's appetite was poor, and he wasn't growing as fast as he should for his age. So she changed doctors. The new one changed one drug (Ritalin) for another (Cylert). She changed doctors, again. This time she found an educational psychologist with a keen interest in nutrition. He recommended discontinuation of the medication, hair analysis, and the basic diet recommended for children by Lendon Smith, M.D., in his exceptional book, Feed Your Kids Right (McGraw Hill, 1979). The hair analysis revealed that Delvin was suffering from iron and zink [sic] deficiencies. In addition, his body needed far

larger quantities of vitamins C and D than he
was getting. The new diet (no sugars, no
additives, no preservatives, no food dyes,
whole grains, white cheeses, peanuts, fish,
chicken, fresh vegetables, and very low sodium)
effected a major change in Delvin's behavior.
Now, with encouragement and a lot of positive
information about his achievements, Delvin was
able to sit down and do his homework at one
sitting for the first time in his life. All this
because a mother persisted. Now she was in a
position to keep talking because Delvin was in a
position to listen and respond. It is very hard
to build a positive self-concept in a youngster
when the messages are not getting through!

In summation, parents in trouble must
objectively look at themselves first. One of the
major causes of sagging self-concept in kids today is the fact that parents simply do not
spend enough time with their children. Another major cause is that parents, during the time
they do spend with their youngsters, send far
more corrective and negative messages to their
kids than positive ones. Perhaps the greatest
cause of sagging self-concept in kids is a sagging self-concept in a parent. As the par-
ent(s) change(s), so will the kid(s).

Secondly, parents must discriminate between what they can change and what they
can't. Then they must go to work finding
positive value in what cannot be changed.
Third, parents must establish firm, consistent,
and clearly communicated house rules and
respond positively when the rules are followed.
The more positive we are about followed rules,
the less we will have to ground, deprive,
admonish, and punish when they are broken.

Finally, we must keep the lines of communication open and keep sending the message of love.

Chapter Seven

TIPS FOR TEACHERS IN TROUBLE

It seems a bleak time for teachers. Discipline, every year for the past ten years, has been named the number one problem facing the schools. Violence along with the problems of busing, bilingualism, special education mainstreaming, teacher strikes, declining enrollments, closing schools, changing neighborhoods, the rise of drug abuse among students, loss of tax bases, loss of federal programs, and many other problems make education a challenging profession and dramatically different from what it was 10-15 years ago.

Certainly by now, you would be disappointed in me if I could not rattle off all the positive aspects of this grim situation.

Well, look at it this way, teachers. Today, there is nothing boring about our profession. Our jobs offer us incredibly demanding challenges about every two minutes. Is it any wonder that occasionally we are carried, like over-stressed air traffic controllers, away from our classrooms on stretchers? Is it any wonder that we suffer a high rate of peptic and duodenal ulcers, heart and cardio-vascular problems, dizziness, nausea, and other stress symptoms, not to mention plain old burnout?

What our communities do not realize (and maybe it is time they should) is that we were given little training in the area of classroom management, and even those of us with years of combat experience in the classroom sometimes have trouble mustering the courage it takes to "face the kids."

Unlike the parents, who rarely have more than two or three at a time to manage, we have thirty-five, forty, and sometimes, on the secondary level, as many as 200 kids in the same room. (Question: How does one build positive self-concepts in 200 kids at the same time? Answer: Very fast, at a speed of 200 mph; say "Good job, nice work, good job, nice work...").

Here are some tips to follow. Each tip has an exercise designed to make your job easier, more rewarding, and more self-concept building for the kids who depend on you for a great education.

Tip One: Seriously Examine and Try at
                  Least One of the Several Excel-
                  lent and Commercially Available
                  Classroom Management Systems.

If you haven't looked lately, or your in-
service committee doesn't have the money, then
investigate and pay yourself for some specific
skills training in effective classroom management. There are two reasons why you must do
this. In the first place, if you are like most
teachers, you haven't been adequately trained
and given specific skills to respond appropriately to today's behavior problems. Secondly,
you cannot begin to build a positive self-concept in kids when your room is in chaos and
you spend your day babysitting. The following
are some programs you may want to investigate:
Dr. Edward Pino's Program, Discipline Strate-
gies That Work (ECA, 1979), is an excellent,
fully mediated package which will give you a
place to start. Dr. James Dobson's book (and
tapes), Dare to Discipline (Tynedale House,
1970), is still an excellent guide for teaching
respect and responsibility to children. Certainly, Dr. William Glasser's approach, Reality
Therapy (Harper and Row, 1976), has helped
thousands of teachers gain control of their lives
in the classroom. Without question, the most
effective of the classroom management systems
is Lee and Marlene Canter's Assertive Discipline
(Canter and Associates, 1976 – available in
book, workbook, film, slide tape, and workshop
format). The Canters' work re-empowers the
classroom teacher to take charge of the educational environment and put him/her in a rela-
tively trouble-free environment in which to
work.

Teachers, once our environment is mostly trouble-free, then our real work begins. The purpose of school is to provide a myriad of real learning opportunities for our kids. The reason we want them to learn is so they lead happy, productive, constructive lives. We do not educate them to be losers at the game of life. If, when they leave us, they have the skills but not the will to use the skills, we have not succeeded.

Exercise for Tip One

Read a book or go to a workshop (preferably both) on the subject of classroom management. Then put into practice for a period of one month the principles you learned. At the end of the one-month period, sit down in a quiet moment and answer these questions:

1. What was good about my classroom management system? (Think positive!)

2. What didn't work? What can I do to fix it?

3. Did the kids understand my rules? Should I change my rules?

4. Did I receive support from the administration and parents on my classroom management system? What can I do to get better support? Did I acknowledge those who did support me? (Was I positive?)

5. Which of my students have benefited the most by my classroom management system? How can I let them know I appreciate their support?

6. Did I structure a positive learning environment with my new management system, or did I succeed only in intimidating the kids with a lot of negative consequences which made them feel like prisoners and me feel like a warden?

7. Does my classroom management system give kids opportunities to win? Have I built in sufficient incentives for them to work by themselves, with me, and with others for the purpose of achieving a goal?

8. Does my new management system help students develop goals and work toward them, so I have greater opportunities to positively respond to the kids?

9. Does my new classroom management system in any way defeat kids or send them negative messages about themselves and serve to destroy developing positive self-concepts?

One final suggestion on Tip One: If you don't like the first classroom management system you try — try another. The best way to find one that works is to ask your colleagues. They will give it to you straight.

Tip Two: Be Good to Yourself

Obviously, you are not going to do a great
job of building a positive self-concept in kids if
your own self-concept is sagging. Here are
some common reasons why a teacher's self-concept sags.

1. Your principal doesn't support you or
    appreciate your work.

2. You are doing more paperwork and
    less teaching than you've ever done,
    and you didn't go to school to be a
    secretary.

3. You are so tired at the end of the
    day, you have no time or energy for
    your own children.

4. The only parents you hear from are
    the ones who do not like what you
    are doing.

5. If it wasn't for one or two kids,
    every day would be great.

6. If it wasn't for one or two kids,
    every day would be terrible.

7. You know your retirement checks will
    be pitifully small, and when you
    retire, social security will be bank-
    rupt. You may have to eat dog food,
    and you haven't found a brand you
    like.

8. If one more kid asks to sharpen his/
    her pencil during a lesson, you will

wrap your hands around his/her throat and squeeze the Charmin.

9. You're afraid to call Tommy's parents because Tommy's father made a pass at one of the other teachers last year (a man).

10. You're afraid to call Consuela's parents because they don't speak English.

11. You're afraid to call Marty's parents because his father is the superintendent.

12. You're afraid to call your own parents because your mother told you not to go into teaching in the first place.

The list goes on and on. I am sure as you read, you thought of a few beauties of your own. Bleak and dismal thoughts and gut-wrenching fears will not help you. Such feelings will leave you with a sense of helplessness and "I can't do it," or "I can't take it anymore." The worst is, "Why am I doing this; no one cares." Hence the tip: Be Good to Yourself. How can you expect anyone to respect you if you do not respect yourself? Here are ten thoughts to start you on the road to rebuilding your own sagging self-concept.

1. You are an important person.

2. Your profession is the most important profession. Without teachers, there aren't any other professions.

3. You have spent thousands, maybe
    hundreds of thousands of hours in
    the grand and demanding company of
    kids; no one knows your kids as well
    as you do.

4. You have special, unique skills and
    insights to impart to kids; they des-
    perately need your human love and
    professional care. They will fail with-
    out you.

5. In many cultures, what you do is con-
    sidered sacred. In some cultures
    (unfortunately not ours anymore)
    people tip their hats and bow to you
    out of respect for your work and
    dedication.

6. You are the professional in whose
    company kids will spend more time
    than with any other professional.
    You are their introduction to the
    world of adults beyond that of their
    parents.

7. For your kids, you are the embodi-
    ment of authority; you represent what
    is good, what is true, and what is
    fair and just.

8. By society, you are asked to play
    more roles than any other profes-
    sional. You are a leader, inspirer,
    minister, dentist, nurse, physician,
    social worker, disciplinarian, mother,
    father, subject-matter expert, human
    and civil rights guardian, government
    representative, artist, crafts person,

committee member, parent-child liaison, jailer, dietician, accountant, and milk money expert. In the main, you play these handily, with a flair, with a sense of humor, and <u>well</u>.

9. You are asked to teach kids who <u>some day</u> will make more money than you, be more powerful than you, make more contributions than you have, change the course of human history, and (even) remove carcinoma from your body with a beam of light. ("Aren't you Mrs. Marks from the Washington school? I remember you. Laser, please!")

10. You are all things to all kids, and more, you are worthy of a special name — a name that (as some say) God's own son was proud to be called by his student, Peter, in the Garden of Gethsemani when he said, "Hail, Teacher."

Exercise for Tip Two

For teachers in the profession longer than
ten years, here is an excellent activity to bol-
ster a sagging self-concept. In a quiet and
reflective moment, construct a list (read old
grade books or yearbooks for memory jogging)
of all the kids you have taught of whom it
could be said you made a significant difference
in their lives. Include on this list all former
students who took the time to write to you after
you taught them; all former and present students who come up to you in the grocery store
to smile and say hello; certainly include all
former students that at the time impressed you
as candidates for the local penitentiary, who
are now distinguished state senators, or
lawyers and gynecologists in Beverly Hills,
Hawaiian real estate developers, and your own
school superintendent. Remember all the things
you said and did to them when they were
"impossible students" and keep on doing it!

For teachers in the profession under ten
years, try the following: In a quiet and reflective moment (and if you don't have many of
these, we have one clue as to why your self-
concept is sagging) construct some realistic and
achievable rewards for yourself (Example: new
dress, glass of rare wine, new golf clubs, etc.)
and make them contingent on an improved performance in an area of your life which needs
attention. (Example: more education course
credit, an improved teacher evaluation, better
interpersonal relations with the administration
or colleagues, etc.) Then stake out a plan for
achieving this goal and get to work. It is
truly wonderful what winning does for the
self-concept!

Remember this lesson from your life the next time you draft an academic or behavioral goal for a kid – nothing helps the self-concept like success – nothing.

Tip Three: Get the Parents Involved Early

There are many reasons why teachers fail
to seek help from parents early. First,
teachers think (erroneously) that calling the
parents of a kid in trouble is an admission of
their own incompetence. Second, teachers
rarely have any ideas when the parent says
"What am I supposed to do with him/her?"
Third, parents often tend to be defensive, and
the teachers do not like battling the defense
mechanisms of parents when they need the
energy to help the kid. Fourth, many teachers
discover from dealing with parents exactly
where the kid learned his/her negative self-
concept and "loser" mentality. Fifth, some
parents are difficult to contact, work long
hours, are never home, don't exist, etc., and
teachers who have expended unrewarded energy
searching for a parent to help, tend to lapse
into a "why bother" posture. Sixth, teachers
frequently have unhappy or frustrating
experiences attempting to work with culturally
different parents. They speak little or no
English, and using an interpreter is awkward,
and done without skill, could lead to an inter-
cultural incident.

The list of reasons for not contacting
parents early when there is trouble goes on,
but the point remains: Teachers have a professional obligation to contact parents early
when there is trouble. So here is a list of
suggestions for making your contact with
parents a positive and rewarding experience for
them as well as yourself because this is the
first step toward unifying the first two
ecologies (see Chapter Three) for the purpose
of building a positive self-concept in a kid.

1. Before you call or send a note to yell
    and scream to parents about what
    their kid did in school, send a
    positive note home telling them what
    an outstanding job their kid did on a
    particular day. Example: "Dear Mr.
    & Mrs. Rodriguez: Rosa Linda was a
    star in mathematics class today.
    Thanks for your support. You must
    be wonderful parents!" Now, tell me
    they are going to be defensive and
    uncooperative next time you need
    their help because Rosa Linda is not
    doing her homework. No way.

2. Be positive about the kid when you
    talk to his/her parents. Remember,
    it is a scary experience for all
    parents to have to talk to their kid's
    teacher. So smile, use humor, make
    them feel relaxed and comfortable by
    stressing the kid's abilities and
    positive virtues.

3. State the problem in very clear
    language. Do not hedge. Don't give
    them the impression that it's nothing
    you can't handle or it's a stage s/he's
    going through, or some other mini-
    mizer. If the kid is stealing, say
    "Kevin is stealing money from other
    kids in the bathrooms." He says,
    "Give me a quarter, or I'll punch
    your lights out."

4. Stress how important the kid's self-
    concept is and that a kid whose self-
    concept includes stealing will continue
    to steal for the rest of his/her life.

5. Propose a plan for developing a more
    positive self-concept for the kid in
    question. Here you have to teach the
    parents to be more positive with Rosa
    Linda or Kevin: you have to teach
    mom and dad how to "catch them be-
    ing good." Most parents do not
    understand this principle. If they
    did, you wouldn't be conferencing
    with them in the first place.

6. Help the parents develop a behavior
    management system at home, one that
    includes rules and positive as well
    as effective negative consequences.
    Stress that it is the positive re-
    sponse, when the kids follow the
    rules, which helps build a positive
    self-concept. Again, parents do not
    understand this principle, or they
    wouldn't be experiencing trouble.

7. When you get evidence that the par-
    ents are responding more positively to
    their kid, get on the phone, write a
    note and (of course) thank them.
    This will help their self-concept, too.

Exercise for Tip Three

Select two of your most troublesome students. Catch them doing something right this week. Send a brief note home to their parents describing the good things you observed. Be sure to thank the parent(s) in advance for "good support." Next time one of these students (or both) does something you do not like, schedule a parent conference and follow the guidelines for a positive parent conference I listed earlier in the chapter. After the conference and a few days of classroom observation, answer these questions:

1. What changes in the kid's behavior have taken place as a result of my meeting with his parents?

2. Have I responded positively when I observed him/her do something I liked?

3. Have I responded positively but in an inappropriate way ("Oh Reggie – [Age 15] – I L-L-L-OVE how you are working now that your mom and dad and I have a little – heh! heh! – understanding,") or at an inappropriate time (in front of the entire class).

4. What messages has the kid been sending me with his/her body language or tone of voice? Are these messages telling me I am the enemy?

5. Did I follow up my conference with his/her parents with a phone call or note designed to be positive with

them for their support and to keep
the lines of communication open
between us?

6. Did the parents follow up on the
    training I gave them? Have they
    positively responded to desirable
    behavior, and have they structured
    their time as well as material items as
    rewards and incentives?

7. Have I been positive, even when dis-
    ciplining this kid, so s/he gets the
    message I care about him/her as a
    person even though there are certain
    behaviors I will not tolerate?

8. How many opportunities, this week,
    has this kid had to win at something
    and feel good about him/herself? How
    could I create more opportunities and
    help to engineer success?

9. How am I feeling about myself since I
    have taken the time, energy, and
    patience to reach out and help par-
    ents and a kid in trouble?

10. How will I feel about myself as I
    begin to see this kid win?

Final note on early parent involvement:
remember, teachers, there's only one thing
more important than winning, and even Vince
Lombardi knew it — that's having the skill to
show somebody else how to win. So spark some
teamwork spirit in those parents. Let them
know you are on their team, and you have a
common goal — the success of their kid. In

reality, teacher, you are not only on their team, you are the coach! So frequently teachers say, "If only the parents knew what they were doing, we wouldn't have this trouble!" Yet, to whom can the parents turn to for help? US! We are the first point of inquiry when parents are in trouble. So we had better be prepared to respond with a winning attitude when they say, "What'll we do now, coach?" Because when we throw in the towel, the match is over, the game is done, and we have lost. When we lose, the kids never have a chance. So, let's go get 'em, team!

Tip Four: Consult Your Colleagues

It is a rare school these days whose faculty and administration are united in their
effort to build positive self-concepts in kids.
Show me a school where the faculty and administration are united in their effort to engineer
positive learning experiences for kids, and I
will show you a school which produces champions every single time. But so many of us in
teaching today are victims of the "little red
schoolhouse syndrome." We think we are all
alone, by ourselves, the kids against us, and
we are incompetent teachers if we cannot do it
all by ourselves. Well, the little red schoolhouse is dead. There is a war zone out there,
and you don't go into a war zone alone. Get
some help. Sit down with your colleagues and
trade tricks on sending kids positive messages.
Ask the veterans, particularly the ones you all
acknowledge are gifted master teachers, and
ask very specific questions about their tech-
niques for helping kids feel good about themselves. The more specific your questions, the
richer and more accurate the response. (You
will likely discover that many gifted teachers,
ironically, have a very difficult time expressing
exactly what it is they do when they deal with
a kid whose self-concept is very negative.
This is understandable when you realize that
very few education courses teach specific skills
for building self-concept in kids, so what your
gifted colleague is doing may be instinctive and
never analytically considered or articulated.)

If you really are on fire to develop self-
concept building skills, spend some time with a
colleague who is a successful and well-respected

athletic coach. You will see positive reinforcement in action. You will see enthusiasm,
desire, motivation, go-go, and win-win mentality at its best. You will see your colleague
smile, laugh, joke, jump up and down, tease in
a constructive, image-building, legend-building
way ("Smith? You want to know about Smith?
Well for openers the kid is a psychic phenomenon. No joke, he has ESP when it comes to
finding the ball carrier. I swear he doesn't
open his eyes! But when he tackles somebody,
I know he has the ball. Kid never misses.")
Did you hear that phrase "kid never misses"?
Well, some other people heard it, too. The
coach made sure of that. Legends are born
this way. Champions are made this way.

Exercise for Tip Four

Sit down with a wise and skillful colleague and ask very specific questions about a specific kid. Find out how your colleague would go about building this kid's self-concept. Take notes and don't say, "It won't work; I tried it." (Don't forget the skills of positive listening and positive talking when working with your colleagues. They need support, too!) Listen particularly for specific rewards your problem kids can earn, like earning the right to be class monitor for Jason, the right to take the attendance cards to the office for Mildred, the right to read first for May Ling, the opportunity to represent the class in a school function for Paul, etc. You will discover from your successful colleagues that among the best rewards for kids are those which carry responsibility. The reason is that handling responsibility well is more than its own reward for kids — it is a major builder of self-confidence.

To summarize tips for teachers in trouble: Teachers today are presented with overwhelming problems and constant stress. Unless we are able to feel good about ourselves and the job we are doing, we will not be effective role models for kids. In order to feel good about ourselves, we must first get some strong classroom management skills. Furthermore, we must not use those skills to trounce kids. Rather, we must develop positive classroom management skills to consistently reinforce kids for doing what we want them to do.

Secondly, we must be good to ourselves by realizing that while society asks us to do a very time-consuming and physically/mentally demanding task, we are special and talented human beings capable of meeting that challenge. We are the backbone of the most moral and good aspects of our society.

Thirdly, we must work with parents, early and often, in order to secure a more positive and self-concept building case for our kids. And we must realize that unless we train the parents to catch the kids being good, no one else will.

Finally, we must realize that we are not alone in our work with kids. We must frequently and assiduously call on our colleagues for new and practical ways of sending positive messages to kids. As teachers we must realize that never was it more apparent that the future is firmly, positively, and irrevocably in our hands, and WE ARE NEEDED.

Chapter Eight

TIPS FOR BUILDING POSITIVE PEER MESSAGES FOR APPROPRIATE BEHAVIOR IN KIDS

You may recall that in an earlier discussion I said that the third ecology (the kid and
his/her friends) is the most powerful ecology of
all. The need to have friends who are loving,
respecting, and approving is great in all of us.
Therefore, much of our behavior is designed to
win the love, respect, and approval of our
friends. This is true of kids as well. In fact,
it is more true of kids than it is of adults
because kids are undergoing tremendous physio-
logical and psychological changes in short
periods of time. They are constantly discover-
ing themselves, rediscovering themselves, and
testing their own limitations. As they play new
roles, experiment with new activities, and adopt
new postures, they embark on a ceaseless
search for acceptance and approval. They
quickly learn that certain behaviors attract
them friends and, in some cases, admirers.
They fear, by the seventh grade, they will be
thought of as "weird," or a "goody-goody" or,
the absolute worst, (at this writing) "queer."
Middle school or junior high teachers, who have
experience teaching at the elementary levels as
well, will tell you that the tremendous difference between elementary and junior high age
kids is the intensification of the socialization
process at the junior high levels. Naturally,
with this intensification comes a need for
greater acceptance as well as greater acces-
sibility to the group. Bathroom humor, popular
in the fifth and sixth grade, begins to fade,
and sexual humor, with great emphasis on boy-
girl differences and the "words" which speak to
these differences, becomes the preoccupation of
the group. The key to survival can be
expressed in the question, "What can I do or
say that will attract to me others who will help
me get my needs met?"

Rather than be threatened by this intensification of socialization in our kids (as parents
frequently are) or punished by it (as teachers
many times are), we must begin to understand
that kids of all ages have strong social needs
and must get them met in order to be happy.
Show me an unhappy kid, and I won't show you
a kid who's worried over bad grades; instead
I'll show you a kid whose friend wants to play
with someone else today, whose friends forgot
to invite her to the party, who was not invited
to the dance, who did not make the team, who
has no date for the prom, whose pimples have
blossomed like roses in June. In short, show
me an unhappy kid, and I'll show you a social
loser in the game of life.

Yet, as parents we fail to teach our children simple (but terribly important) socialization skills and worse, as teachers, we system-
atically punish them for being social, because,
teachers say, they choose to be social at the
wrong times. Many times we fail to teach kids
the minimum skills they need to survive in a
world of others who need as much or more reinforcement than they do. One reason we do is
that we are so busy attending to our own social
needs, we forget the needs of our kids. How
important it is for kids to learn the difference
between people who love you for you and people
who love you because you fit their agendas.
How important it is for our kids to learn the
difference between people who are "givers" and
people who are "takers" – between people who
are "helpers" and people who are "users."

Until our kids learn these "life" lessons,
they are prey to their own needs for love,

acceptance, and approval. The world is filled
with predators, some of whom act consciously
and others who unwittingly destroy and hurt
many of the people they touch.

All of this boils down to a critical skill our
kids must have in order to survive in the
strange world we live in today. The skill is
picking and choosing friends. Most parents, as
they do with matters of discipline, react to the
friends their children choose: they either like
them, or they don't. Few parents go beyond
the stage of expressing their likes and dislikes
until some trouble develops. "You were caught
what? Shoplifting! Oh my God, I don't believe
this. You were with that Maxwell girl, weren't
you? I told you she was bad news, didn't I?"
"That Maxwell girl" may very well be bad news,
mom, but tell me this: did you ever sit down
with your daughter and have a non-threatening
and plainly instructive chat about what to look
for in picking a friend?

Teachers, who spend many hours of their
days observing friendship and patterns of
influence among kids, are an excellent resource
for parents who want to know about their children's friends. We watch so many "nice kids"
in school come under the irresistible influence
of others who send those powerful "I like you;
you're a neat person" messages for the wrong
reasons. Kids who normally draw so little of
that reinforcement from home and teachers at
school are so vulnerable to that message of support they will do anything, virtually anything,
to improve, augment, and maintain those messages of regard from their friends.

Consider, too, that this third ecology includes a special group called siblings. Siblings are special peers in that they participate in the home ecology, may participate in the school ecology (depending on age difference), and participate in the peer ecology as well. Instinctively, parents recognize the special place occupied by siblings – "You keep an eye on your brother, understand? I don't want him in any more trouble." Siblings are the members of the peer ecology over which parents should realize they have a measure of control.

My point is that the place to begin is for parents and teachers to realize that we have the potential for exercising much greater influence in the peer ecology than we commonly recognize. Here are some tips for parents, to be followed by tips for teachers, for the purpose of exercising more influence over the kinds of messages our kids' friends are sending them about their behavior.

Parent Tip One: Know   Your   Children's
                     Friends.

Go out of your way to get them in your
life, if only for brief but meaningfully shared
experiences. Family parties, picnics, outings,
camping trips, special occasions send out the
message: you are welcome here. Send them
the positive messages you are sending your
children, and you will get to know them well.
In fact, if you go overboard on the positives
for your children's friends, you will need an
addition on the house. They will never go
home!

Parent Tip Two: Do Not Cross-Examine Your
                     Children's Friends.

If they suspect that they are invited for
the purpose of information-gathering and scru-
tiny, they will evaporate like dew on a desert
morning. Questions like, "What does your
father do for a living, Janet?" may be harmless
enough, but the game of "twenty-questions"
grows old for kids, and they get a very negative message from interrogation.

Parent Tip Three: Watch   For   the   Behavior
Your   Children's   Friends
Encourage   in   Your   Children;   Watch   For   the   Behavior   Your   Children   Encourage   in   Their   Friends.

Understanding   the   motivating   factors
behind   everyday   decisions   your   children   make
is easier when you realize that they are partici-
pating in a circle of friends and acquaintences
which has a behavior code of its own.   This
code may embrace some of your own values,
then again, it may embrace values foreign and
threatening to your own.   Observing the messages your children's friends send them will not
only   help   you   understand   your   children's
behavior, it will help you assess the relative
strength of their self-concepts as they invariably   compare   themselves   to   their   friends.
Remember, they have to be happy in their own
world.   In   order   to   survive   without   serious
scars, psychological traumas, and emotional set-
backs, they have to follow the rules of their
own world.   Conflicts with you may arise when
your world's values have no meaning or have a
negative meaning for your children.   One way
to understand their world is to be vigilant about
messages of regard which they exchange.   If
they reward one another for wearing certain
shirts, jeans, blouses, or shoes because they
are "in," then we must understand that as parents we are presented with an opportunity.
Most parents miss the opportunity.   Because
the "in" clothers inevitably cost more, some
parents   are   outraged.   "Why   should   I   pay
$21.95 for this shirt because it has that silly
logo, when I can buy the same thing at K-Mart
for $8.95?"

The "when I was your age" lecture may
very well justify to you why you refuse to submit to pressure; it doesn't help them in their
attempt to fit into their own world. Their
friends and acquaintances may very well bruta-
lize them for living by your values in their
world. Now, of course, if their self-concept is
so strong and self-assured that they can laugh
in the face of peer derision, then you have
done a great job and very well may have a
trend setter for a son or daughter. But if
they lack the self-assurance to effectively deal
with peer derision (kids can be very cruel;
they learn it from us), then you have set them
up. They walk into a potentially harmful world
defenseless and wearing red flags and the scent
of the victim. After getting chewed-up,
roughed-up, and hurt by their peers, they will
develop a rather sophisticated set of defense
mechanisms. Some of these will irritate you.
"How come he spends so much time in his room
lately?" "All she does is come home, get something to eat, and go into her room and listen to
her stereo." "She just will not eat. I suppose
she's worried about being overweight. But,
Lord, she's thin as a stick. She refuses to
eat. When she does, I think she makes herself
throw-up." "He just quit school. And he was
getting good grades. One day he just quit."

Now, I am not suggesting to parents that
they buy every little whim, give in on every
issue, turn over the checkbook to the kid – far
from it. I am suggesting that understanding
the circumstances behind the behavior (particularly the peer pressure) gives you an excellent opportunity to build a positive self-concept
in a youngster. Witness: "Jeffrey, I understand the situation. All your friends wear

alligator shirts. You like them, too. But they cost six and a half dollars more than the same shirt without the alligator. Here's the deal. I think you are number one, and you should wear the best. So, you will have to earn the difference between the costs of the shirts. I pay a dollar an hour for window cleaning, leaf raking, and babysitting your brother and sister."

Now Jeffrey has an opportunity to wear the clothes he wants to feel comfortable among his friends – furthermore, he has great incentive to work! His shirts take on a new meaning. They now symbolize his responsibility to himself. Do you think you will find them crumpled in a ball in the bottom of his closet? More than likely, you will find the shirts he spent six and a half hours each working to get hung neatly in a closet or folded in his drawer. Before long he will request, mom, that you iron them (even though they are perma-press). Remembering the formula for positive self-concept, you take the opportunity to say, "I am impressed that you care enough about your appearance to want ironed shirts. Since I don't have the time to iron them myself, I would be happy to teach you to iron them." He will – of course. Again, another opportunity to feel good about himself, and haven't you taught him a wonderful lesson about life? You want it; you work for it. All this because instead of screaming, "I don't care what your friends are wearing, I'm not etc., etc." or saying, "Iron perma-press? You need your head examined!" or worse, "Sure I'll iron them for you, honey." By realizing the messages Jeffrey's friends are sending him, we help Jeffrey to win.

But his friends aren't the only ones sending messages; he's sending them back. By

watching these, you will learn an enormous
amount about yourself. Is he mean to his
friends? Moody with his friends? Tease them
to the point of pain? Use them for his own
ends? Or is he supportive of their needs and
sharing? Is he polite with them? Does he
encourage them to try? Does he help them win?
Whatever messages he sends, mom and dad,
remember this: how he treats them is exactly
what he learned from you.

Parent Tip Four: Periodically Discuss Your
                    Children's   Friends   With
                    Your Children.

Now, the worst thing you can do is give
the impression that you are evaluating and making decisions about your kid's friends. Don't
do it. What you want is for the kid to have
the skill to evaluate and make decisions about
his/her friends. Because friendship is so
important to all of us, it has become almost a
"sacred cow." Yes, we believe it is a basic
human right to choose our own friends. Of
course it is. Friends who hurt us for their
own ends are not friends. Face it, mom and
dad, it's one of life's toughest lessons. Just
who are our friends, anyway? So your discus-
sions with your kids about their friends should
give your kids the freedom to draw their own
conclusions. You can lead the discussion to
cover points about goals, objectives, healthy
activities, dangerous activities, and don't forget
those self-concept messages: friends who send
self-concept crippling messages are not friends,
and when they are lovers, the relationship will
never last. If by chance it does, it can never
be healthy, and unhealthy relationships have a
way of producing troubled kids. Thus, the
cycle of defeat is complete. By responding positively to each other and our children, we boldly
break that destructive cycle.

Tips For Teachers

   As teachers, we have a major advantage
over parents when it comes to observing peer
message systems shape kids. We see it happen-
ing every day in our classrooms, in the halls,
in the recess yard and cafeteria, in the parking
lot, and at "the gathering place for trouble" –
almost every school has one. We regularly and
daily observe the social interaction of the kids.
In fact, we see so much of it, we become
inured to the psychological destruction that may
happen under our noses. We hear them "cut
up" each other, listen to cruel and judgmental
nicknames, observe them in potentially dangerous and image-compromising behavior, and we
say or do nothing.

   We can channel the energy they have to
hurt each other into activities which will teach
them mutual respect. Furthermore, we can
structure those activities to teach them to be
more supportive of each other with activities
which enhance rather than interfere with our
lessons and actually train the kids to send self-
concept building messages to each other. Here
are some tips to help you design such activities
for your particular classroom and school.

Teacher Tip One: Make Rules Which Prohibit
the Exchange of Overt
Negative Messages Among
the Kids.

Beyond the obvious rules like "no fighting," "no name-calling or teasing," and "do not destroy the property of others," you can add rules like "no nicknames," "no obscene language or gestures," or "say or do nothing which could hurt or offend another person's feelings."

Once you have developed these rules, enforce them, and don't say "we can't do that at our school" and sound like a loser. Be a winning teacher, and do something about it when Marvin calls Carrie "the lip" and everybody laughs. Remember if you do not enforce the rules, your rules are a waste of time. Also remember that the best way to enforce the rules is to catch a kid observing them. "Marvin, I noticed that you called everyone today by their first name. I appreciate it, Marvin. You're super!"

Teacher Tip Two: Don't Punish The Group
                    For The Errors of A Few.

It seems obvious to include this tip, but
many teachers use the technique of punishing
the group for the mistakes of a few. The
Marines may claim this technique builds group
spirit, but it doesn't. It does lead to the
group, behind the barracks and at night,
throwing a blanket over the head of the
offender and beating him to a bloody pulp. In
schools this technique leads to the exchange of
negative and self-concept shattering messages.

In response to this tip, some teachers will
say, "But what do you do if you don't know
who did it?" The answer to this question lies
in the following illustration of group rewards:

Pino, Glasser, the Canters (see
Chapter Seven), and others all detail
excellent models for classwide reward systems. The point of their use is that they
unequivocally promote group collaboration,
cohesion, and the exchange of positive
information between students for doing
what you want them to do. Example: a
teacher who offers the class a reward of
listening to their favorite radio station for
five minutes at the end of class if they
earn forty "bonus" points during the
class, has a very sophisticated (and easy-
to-execute) behavior management tool at
his/her disposal. The kids win these
"bonus" points at the sole discretion of the
teacher. S/he awards them as s/he
catches kids in the act of following the
rules and making contributions to the
general welfare of the class. Students

whose peers previously "egged them on"
by laughing and generally admiring them
for destroying the learning atmosphere,
now send them glances of approval as they
win bonus points toward "the prize." Of
course, they must win, and they must
want the prize. You, teacher, engineer
the win by awarding the final point (to the
worst behavior problem, of course), ten
seconds prior to the last five minutes of
the day or class period. Now, the worst
behavior problem, who is the one with the
lowest self-concept, naturally is cheered
by his/her friends for doing what you
wanted him/her to do. If you are clever
enough to offer a "Three-minute bonus on
the radio" if there are no rules broken
during the class, then you do not have to
"see" them to catch the rule breaker.
When you hear the disruption you
announce, calmly, the loss of the bonus.
The kids will look directly at the offender
and you will know who caused the trouble.
This way you monitor the class without
"watching" them. Of course, whatever
you do to the offender is not nearly the
punishment s/he receives as the class
stares in silence in his/her direction. If
you haven't seen this phenomenon in action
(and I can't imagine you haven't), it is a
graphic demonstration of the power of the
peer ecology. Because you are a positive
teacher, you will strive to help them win.
(I suggest that the student whose disruption lost the bonus be the student whose
behavior earns the last few bonus points
for the first part of the reward so s/he
is redeemed in the eyes of his/her
friends.)

Teacher Tip Three: Use   Peer   Teaching.

    I am astonished at how little my colleagues
rely on one of the greatest and most easily
obtainable resources in our classrooms today –
the kids themselves. A lot of reliable research
on peer teaching says it is a highly effective
teaching technique. What the research doesn't
point out is what peer teaching does for self-
concept. In the first place, it allows the
teacher to publicly recognize students with
special subject matter knowledge and skills
(positive messages from the first eoclogy).
Secondly, it allows the student to tell his/her
parents of the special recognition as s/he
prepares the lesson at home. Of course, positive parents will respond appropriately (positive
messages from the second ecology). Thirdly, it
permits the student to help his/her classmates
to learn from one of their own, which is
especially rewarding when a certain prize has
been offered if all students score above a certain grade on the test, complete a special
assignment, etc. (positive messages from the
third ecology). Of course, the teacher, freed
from the pressure of delivering the lesson is
free to pay more attention to the process of
positive self-concept development, which, as
any teacher will tell you, is one of the greatest
joys of our profession, and on this point, I end
the final chapter of this book, but please do
read on!

EPILOGUE: NEVER TOO LATE TO BEGIN

I have to believe as William Faulkner said so well when he accepted the Nobel Prize for literature, "Man will endure." I have to believe that we will endure because we have the power to change, and I also believe that we can never change the behavior of someone else unless we ourselves are willing to change. When we demonstrate our ability to change to kids, we teach them a powerful lesson about life. We teach them that they have the power to do virtually anything they want to do – be anything they want to be.

Kids are forever. They are at once our joy and our frustration. They are Hamlet's mirror held up to ourselves. For nothing angers us more than seeing our own faults in our children. Nothing pleases us more than hearing another say something nice about our kids. Because they grow up with us and we – is it not true? – grow up with them, we know each other's sources for pleasure and pain. Who can hurt you more than your mother? And who, with a word or two or a sentence in a letter, can make you weep silent tears of joy? Why, in the cartoon, does the psychiatrist thoughtfully stroke his beard and say, "Tell me about your mother"?

Why, teacher, does the memory of a certain student stay with us forever? Don't we get that special shot of joy when they come back after long years with that look-what-I've-done-with-my-life-and-thank-you look? It needs no words.

I have tried in this book to speak to you from my heart and say things I have spent long hours thinking about, reading about, talking about, teaching about, probably – you'll smile – preaching about because as an athlete, teacher, parent, and professional helper, I see winners and losers every day. And while they all pretty much look the same, they do not act the same, and they certainly do not speak the same language. The language of lose is replete with the words "I can't," "I won't," and "why bother?" The language of win uses words like "I can," "I will," and "why not?"

The language of lose in the mouth of a derelict, convict, or terrorist is understandable, indeed. But the language of lose in the mouth of a kid is crushing. When you hear it, you always wonder what a toll forty, fifty, or sixty years of losing will take on this kid as well as on the innocent bystanders in the accident of his/her life. It is we who teach them how to talk.

Now, the language of win is music in the mouth of a child. It first tinkles like a wind harp in a light breeze; it is a prelude to the thundering overture of a great life filled with the sound and the fury signifying something. That something is why we must believe we will endure. That hope is always born in our children. Let us teach them the language of win. Let us feed their souls with "I can" and "I will" and "why not?" Let the language of win help them grow strong in their own eyes. For it is never too late to begin. For them and the generations which follow, we can offer no greater gift.

Thank you for reading my book and GO GET 'EM.

If you wish additional copies of

Breakfast for Champions

fill out the form below and mail to:

J. Zink, Inc.
1101 John Street
Manhattan Beach, CA   90266
(213) 545-1031

Please add postage and packaging
charges of $1.05 per book ordered

$6.95 each

California residents add 6% sales tax.

****

I would like _____ copies

of Breakfast for Champions.   Here is my check

for _____ made payable to   J. Zink, Inc.

Name _____

Address_____

(City)   (State)   (Zip)

(A 15% discount is available on
orders of 10 or more copies.)

****